Rocks

Make the

River

Sing

For Jacque ↵

Breathe deep...

Eileen Thornburgh

Eileen Thornburgh

ISBN: 10:1500156140
ISBN-13: 978-1500156145

Dedication

This book is written in loving memory of my parents, Betty and Jim, in honor of my sisters, Harriet and Louise, and dedicated to my courageous husband, John.

Acknowledgement

I thank Jackie Shellworth, friend, educator, editor, and photographer, for her patience, her insistence, her discretion, and her vision.

I thank Harriet and Louise for aiding my memory and correcting my errors, in writing and in recall.:

Praise for *Rocks Make the River Sing*

"Eileen Thornburgh gives us a memoir in stories and poems. Her stories read like poetry. Her poems sing like hymns. Family and nature. Life and death. *Rocks Make the River Sing* makes a reader believe."

Barbara Morgan, NASA Astronaut

****

"*Rocks Make the River Sing* is not a memoir that exposes the family skeletons. Instead it is a memoir that celebrates family with wistful affection and gentle irony. Eileen Thornburgh's childhood in Newport Beach was as serene as the surrounding beaches, and her adult life in Idaho exploring the deserts and mountains with her husband has been equally fulfilling. She has had her tragedies, enduring a bout with breast cancer and yet turning her struggle and cure into one of the funniest moments in the book when she smuggles drinks into BSU football games inside her new bra. This typifies Eileen's attitude toward life. She is a survivor as the book's final vignette about a moose hunt that goes perilously wrong attests. This is a fine memoir that women will love and men will find surprisingly engaging. "

Jim Irons, Idaho's Writer-in-Residence (2001-2004)

****

"Eileen Thornburgh offers a rich tapestry of writings that celebrate that which she holds precious in life; family, nature, music, teaching and adventure. Her eloquent prose and poetry address subjects that range from the super- real to the more elusive areas of memory, loss, survival, inspiration and love. *Rocks Make the River Sing* communicates her independent perspective that is richly informed by a keen intellect, an open heart, compassion, courage and a generous dose of humor."

Kevin Kirk, composer, jazz pianist

****

"Nature is a good educator. Eileen Thornburgh's writings reflect this while carrying us along on her thoughts and struggles of life. To us 'trap boys' at the South Coast Gun Club, Eileen's parents set standards for us to live by, which now our own children inherit. Yet times change, as evidenced by her poem Thank You, Crow. While Eileen appreciates the crow for waking her to see a dawn, her old man would have 'dusted it' for the noise. Eileen writes with heart and an interest in life and nature, lasting gifts from her parents."

John Doughty, JD's Big Game Tackle, Newport Beach (since 1976)

****

Rocks Make the River Sing

Under and over and around the rocks— the river sings

of joy

of pain

of fear

of hope--

Songs of love

The river—your river,

Gentle, furious, peaceful, thundering

Crashing over boulders of grief and disappointment

Swirling in eddies of calm and satisfaction,

Air and life in bubbles and froth,

Strength and patience in pebbles and sand,

A harmony of river and rocks

Its music is life; tumultuous, serene,

Flowing to a rhythm that is singularly your own.

Breathe deep and smile...

Your river sings.

∞ ∞

Love After Life

Someone to Watch Over Me

there's a somebody I'm longing to see

They met on New Year's Eve, 1945. World War II
had just ended—another war to end all wars—and
Jimmy, the sailor, wanted Jim, the submariner, to
meet his 17-year-old sister, Betty. Betty could
laugh, sing, jitterbug, and best of all, she could
make the old upright piano in a ramshackle
clapboard house jump to Stan Kenton's music.
What better way to bring in the New Year and with
it peace and prosperity. Betty, a beautiful,
voluptuous young woman and Jim, a tall,
handsome young man, fell in love before midnight
and married before spring, just three weeks shy of
her 18th birthday.

As a kid, Jim bodysurfed the beaches of Newport
Beach, probably during school hours. He had been
encouraged by the Nuns to leave the Catholic
school in which his divorced mother had worked

so hard to get him enrolled. "Question authority" was not a catch phrase in the 1930's; however, questioning anything and everything was how Jim lived his life.

He did not enjoy the constraints of Catholicism, and the Church's disapproval of his mother's divorce did not improve his opinion of organized religion. Transferring to a public high school allowed him more freedom, and he did not squander those opportunities. The thrill of conquering waves called to him on a daily basis. Pool halls and hot rods were his other pastimes, far surpassing school desks and English Composition. As many did in wartime, Jim left high school before graduating and joined the Navy.

****

Betty and her three brothers and little sister grew up in that small house on the edge of the bean fields of Fountain Valley, just a few miles north of Newport on the Pacific Coast Highway. Their mom raised chickens in the two acre backyard. The farmer's fields were the children's preferred playground, and running through the insecticide spray from the crop dusters was a highlight. Their father was an immigrant from Ireland and brought with him his love of both the Catholic Church and whiskey.

Betty's parents had started out in Louisiana. When the whiskey got to be too much and too often, her mom packed up her little three little boys and took a train to the beaches of California. She gave birth to Betty shortly after arriving in Fountain Valley. Eventually, she let Grandpa move back in. Grandma ironed, tended the chickens, and ran her little café. Grandpa worked in the oil fields, went to church, and still drank his wages.

Betty wondered how her father could be a man of faith yet be abusive to his children when he drank too much. When Betty was thirteen, she missed her period. After just starting puberty, missing a period should not have been a big deal. But when Betty's father heard her tell her mother her period was late, he was so angry he hit Betty and broke her collarbone. Betty had no idea what could possibly cause a late period. She was frightened she had done something so wrong her father would beat her, but did not know what it could be. Sex education was not a part of public education in the 1930's and 40's. Apparently, Catholicism didn't address it either.

Despite being poor, the family continued to put money in the Sunday collection basket. When their furniture was taken by bill collectors, Betty's mom began saving her ironing money. The first thing she bought back was the piano. When Fleming Allan wrote "Behind Those Swinging Doors", a rousing song about a father drinking in a saloon instead of supporting his family, Betty played that tune on the piano with obvious joy and indignant passion.

For the first 17 years and the next 40, hardship never got her down. Her work ethic and music gave her strength and happiness. And Jim, that *someone she was longing to see*, gave her someone to love.

Instead of finishing high school, Betty decided she needed to work at her mother's café on the Balboa Peninsula near the boat docks and Balboa Ferry. Coffee at Ruth's Café was five cents, and apple pie was two bits, the slangy equivalent to one quarter. Tips were hard earned, but the collection basket helped the poorer, so Betty continued her Sunday service. Peace was in the air and life was good. Better for those whose fathers were sober, but still in America and after the war, life was good.

Blue Skies

never saw the sun shining so bright,

never saw things going so right

In April of 1946, Betty and Jim lacked diplomas, but they were eager for work, eager for marriage, eager to start a family, eager to buy a home and a car...of course they could do these things. Why not? They were young Americans and they were in love. Of course they could.

Fruits of the post-war boom wore cloth diapers and drank mother's milk. Children were blessed with grateful parents—fathers grateful for having won the war and mothers grateful for having husbands with all their limbs. And so it was for Jim and Betty. The California coast held onto their hearts. It was a natural decision to work and raise a family there.

Over their first six years, Jim and Betty bought an old car that boasted curb feelers and wind-wings, and a stucco home to call their own with $50 per month payments. Dad's mechanical ability and Mom's financial experiences made a successful partnership. They saved their money and bought a home on the Balboa Peninsula, and leased harbor front land for Jim's Muffler Service on the Pacific Coast Highway. Dad installed mufflers while Mom took care of the accounting and raised three daughters.

First came the fair skinned daughter, Harriet; red-haired, responsible, and mature by the age of six. As a baby, Harriet was always dressed in her bonnet with her red curls tumbling out around the edges. Carrots were a close match to the color of her hair. With her stubby little nose white with zinc oxide and her cheeks speckled with freckles, Harriet was the neighborhood darling.

Louise, the olive skinned daughter came next. Finally out of the womb and on her own, her true colors emerged, healthy and demanding. She was stunning and distinctive with the darkest brown eyes that turned to black when she thought she had been misunderstood. Louise was analytical and headstrong by the age of two.

Then Sweet P; Eileen. That would be me. I was the auburn-haired, freckled, wild daughter, the cross between Harriet's fair and Louise's dark, and the antithesis of responsible and thoughtful. The P in Sweet P stands for Pain, and I joyfully lived up to that name with my sisters until age 16. Life was good, especially for me.

Itsy Bitsy Teenie Weenie
Yellow Polka-Dot Bikini

so in the water she wanted to stay

Our first home on the peninsula was just a few houses away from the ocean. Back then, railroad tracks ran along the ocean front to the fisherman's wharf and piers. Mom showed us the magical properties of beach sand. She helped us pour sand along the top of a train track, and when the train rolled over it the sand turned to super soft powder. We carried handfuls of the precious powder home in our pockets. Mom also taught us to place a penny on the center of one of the rails so when the train went by it would smash the penny flat. Because of my little copper treasures, I knew I was rich and courageous.

Our parents started the muffler shop in the 1950's. The back of the shop adjoined some boat docks jutting out into the harbor across from Lido Isle. In those days, Newport Beach was growing, but it was not yet a millionaire's paradise. It was a coastal town with bays, islands, ferries, piers, fish wharfs, a jetty, and gorgeous beaches with 360 days of sun and five days with fog before noon. The shop smelled of salt water, sea spray, and automotive oil. It was full of greasy tools to play with and chunks of steel to stack and topple. It was heaven with a great view.

In the 60's, they moved the muffler shop to Newport Boulevard near The Ancient Mariner, making room for The Stuffed Shirt Restaurant on PCH. After ten years, the days of sitting on the docks watching the hydroplane races and getting drenched by their rooster-tails were over.

The new shop was larger than the old one, so our dad bought an old upright piano and Mom stuck tacks into the felts. The metal tacks made songs played on the shop piano sound honky-tonk, which perfectly matched Dad's fun-loving personality. His fingers, large from hard work and heavy lifting, barely fit between the keys, yet he would fill that muffler shop with Leroy Anderson's folklore song "The Irish Washerwoman". The chipped white keys, smudged with car grease, were almost as dark as the black keys. Customers would comment that Jim's was the only automotive shop in California where they could get a muffler with music.

The new shop was a great playground, with two hydraulic hoists. We could raise the ramps to the top and then swing down on the shop's roof supports to the ground. It was only when I turned 13 did I learn this was unseemly behavior for a young lady. Pox on the customer who shamed me with that assessment. My dad had always just warned me to be careful not to break the car hoist.

My dad taught me about exhaust systems and a little bit about welding. I don't know who was more proud, Daddy or me, when I installed a glass pack muffler and welded the tailpipe on a Chevy Nova. We were so fortunate to have a father that loved learning and teaching, and held no gender bias.

Mom taught us to swim in the Newport Harbor at a little beach just four houses down from our second peninsula home. She thrived on the beach and in the bay, staying healthy and strong. When some landowners attempted to secure private title to the shore, Mom fought the proposal through the city's planning and zoning, and she won. The little beach would stay open to the public.

Mom was not only knowledgeable and articulate, but she was right. Our family called it Mom's Beach. It is about 50 feet wide and 20 feet from sidewalk to water. Newport has another beach across from the Jetty at the opening of the harbor called Mother's Beach. I don't know whose mother that beach was named for, but it is beautiful, with rocky cliffs and spectacular views of the bay and the ocean. But my mom's beach is my favorite.

Happy Trails

just sing a song and bring the sunny weather

Roy Rodgers' home was on a nearby island, but our little two-story was comfortable, welcoming, and in a healthy neighborhood for children. We could walk to the Fun Zone, ride the Ferris wheel, and catch the ferry that crossed the harbor to Balboa Island. Bare feet, suntans, and dripping syrup from a chocolate-covered banana made Newport a kid's paradise.

Our elementary school playground was the sandy shore of the Pacific Ocean. Hands-on biology was just outside our classroom doors. Whales occasionally beached and died, small fish constantly washed ashore, birds feasted, sand crabs scurried, and life and death were evident with every walk across the sand. Science was everywhere and our family discussions every night at the dinner table centered around thought-provoking possibilities.

Just down the street from our school was the Catholic Church. Mom was still cautiously religious, while Dad was less than enthused, probably part of that question authority attitude. Mom sewed beautiful Easter outfits every year and we shopped for matching gloves, hats, and patent leather shoes. That was the one time every year that Daddy went to church with us. Mom also sewed our confirmation dresses; white, lacy, and full skirted. We girls loved the new outfits. Veils and fluffy slips hinted at future weddings, and we were excited to be the center of attention.

The underlying beliefs of the Catholic faith were not discussed at our dinner table. We were taught to question, to think critically, and to read between the lines. Outright analysis of the existence of God would come as we matured, once we already had a respectable foundation laid before us. We were not told how to think, but we were definitely encouraged to think. Blind faith, whether it was religion or politics, was not an option.

A few years after I went through confirmation, a priest came to visit our house. He had determined that since Mom and Dad had been married in the Las Vegas Gretna Green Chapel and not the Catholic Church, we three daughters, now with ages between 10 and 15, were illegitimate. After informing Mom of our bastardly status and that the only way to remedy this unfortunate situation was for Jim and Betty to marry properly, Mom promptly evicted the priest from our home.

That ended any expectation of mandatory Sunday church attendance. We could go if we wanted, but Mom told us not to be ashamed in front of any church's official, ever. It wasn't long after that clergy visit she chose to stop attending services.

Dad said he believed in the possibility of a supreme being, but he wasn't convinced that being inside an expensive cathedral was the best way to come to know of his existence. Mom believed in the Catholic God, but she was more interested in helping humanity than helping the Church coffers. Organized obedience did not sit well with her, when there were so many people in need of food, clothing, shelter, and freedom.

As we three girls matured, we chose to postpone any definitive decision regarding Catholicism, supreme beings, and the good works necessary to attain a later life in heaven. We certainly questioned reincarnation, departing souls, and eternal damnation, but when the sun is shining and the waves keep rolling to shore, existential analysis didn't demand our attention. The sciences of botany and zoology were surrounding us. We were immersed in the reality of natural systems, currents, and tides. The fact that a Catholic Church graced the shore of the peninsula was accepted as architecture. God was certainly not part of our equation, and we felt no lack for it.

They Can't Take That Away From Me

the way you change my life

We spent our childhood and teenage years near the ocean and Newport Harbor. It was important to Mom that her three daughters take piano lessons. She wanted us to learn to read music, but even more, she wanted us to love its rhythms and poetry. Piano lessons were expensive, especially on a blue-collar salary. Mom sewed our clothes and could cook hamburger a hundred different ways. She took a community class in cake decorating and baked beautiful birthday cakes for each of us every year. Music lessons were essential, more so than store-bought blouses or steak or cake, and in her view, lessons were not a luxury.

Our piano teacher's home was on a hill overlooking Newport Harbor with the grand piano opened to vaulted ceilings, picture-window walls, and the gorgeous blue sky beyond. Loving music came naturally, with a piano at home and one at Daddy's shop, and the weekly lessons over the bay.

Despite not having finished high school herself, it was imperative her daughters be independent and able to support themselves. Mom came by that philosophy naturally, as her own mother could barely feed and clothe her family, in no small part by having a loving but alcoholic husband.

While in high school, Mom and Dad would ask us, "What college are you going to go to?" We were never asked "if" we wanted to go to college. That was a given. Mom said, "No one can ever take your education away from you." Thinking, questioning, studying the tangible and the intangible, the quantitative and the qualitative, and always giving an honest analysis were the foundations of our education.

No Other Love Have I

locked in your arms I'll stay

Mom knew she had a hard-working, devoted husband, and Dad knew he was married to a loving wife who cooked for him, sewed for him, cleaned and cared for him. For years Daddy brought home his daily work receipts in his left shirt-pocket. Sitting at the dinner table, he would empty that pocket of the yellow carbon papers and calculate his earnings out loud, while I got out pencil and paper and did the math. Mom would be cooking dinner and the house would be filled with piano music. He never once stopped off at any local bars, understanding very well that if he did, he would lose the finest woman and the best wife any man could ever hope to know.

Harriet inherited Mom's curvaceous figure and bloomed into a 6' tall, gorgeous red-head. She was the studious daughter, an honor student and national merit scholar. Foreign language came easily to her, and she was the favorite of the German Club. Harriet loved and understood math, breaking gender barriers still prevalent in the mid 1960's. One of her favorite piano pieces was Jack Fina's "Bumble Boogie". It was fast paced, exciting, and a mathematical challenge she won.

Louise was the dusky, alluring socialite. Also tall, she was model thin, high cheek bones, with dark, dark eyes. The in-crowd of Newport Harbor High School welcomed her as one of their own. She joined Drill Team, Modern Dance Club, and dated the most popular seniors. Mom taught Louise how to sew at a young age, and Louise put that skill to use creating fashions from Vogue magazine. She was beautiful, intelligent, and had ambitions to be a dynamic attorney. She could play the piano version of "Ebb Tide" with emotion bordering on heartbreak. Like Mom and Dad, Newport's coast was in her, heart and soul.

And then there was Sweet P. The role of scholar was taken, as was the popular, social, beauty queen persona. I was a shy, average student with a flat chest. What else could I do except rebel. In the 1960's, girls were required to take home economics classes, but I would have preferred to learn to be a better welder than make baking powder biscuits. Louise was already an accomplished seamstress, so learning to make an apron with contrasting pockets did not interest me.

I chose to avoid being compared to my sisters by not being interested in school. During pep rallies, I hung out in the bathroom with the smokers. I didn't smoke, but I liked their company better than being herded like sheep onto the gymnasium bleachers and screaming of false school spirit. I felt obligatory cheering was patently insulting. By graduating months before the prom or grad night at Disneyland, I didn't have to worry about maybe not having a date. I pounded out Jerome Kern's "Ol' Man River" with a vengeance when I got to *tote that barge, lift that bale, get a little drunk and you'll land in jail.* I wasn't angry, just a little lost.

One of our Dad's interests was rifle and pistol shooting. He taught all three of us how to shoot, but I was the daughter that took up the sport. As I entered high school, Daddy sold his muffler shop and took a job as General Manager of the South Coast Gun Club. He had been doing mechanic work for 20 years, and he was ready for a new challenge. Mom had already been working for the gun club for several years as the secretary treasurer. She did all the hiring, firing, bookkeeping, and scheduling: a one-woman Personnel and Accounting Department. Daddy was just a figurehead, but she never told him that.

The gun club was where I spent my weekends, joining the smallbore rifle team and becoming an accurate shooter while getting to spend time with the guys on the team and the gun club's young male employees. I loved being the only female on the team and being a better marksman than many of my boyfriends. I was accepted, popular, and dated guys who loved the outdoors, just like I did.

When he was still running the muffler shop, Daddy would take his days off to either go to the gun club or take a week during deer hunting season and head to Idaho. Even though he taught us to target shoot, we seldom got to go hunting with him, because the seasons conflicted with school calendars. Education was more important than hunting, in our parents' eyes.

When I did get to go hiking through the hills looking for wild animals, I knew I had found my passion. I think Daddy knew by instilling in me a love of the outdoors, he was creating a hunting partner for some young man, for life. He knew not many women would forego lovely dresses for hiking boots and skinning knives, and he wanted to make sure I had my opportunity. My rebellion was actually his gift to me. I have always laughingly called myself my father's only "son". Because he saw no gender roles, I was allowed to strike my own path, with confidence .

Sunrise, Sunset

swiftly fly the years

The ocean is a central focus of life on the coast. Our school lives and our vacations revolved around the ocean's seasons. Our high school nickname was The Tars, and our yearbook was The Galleon. Restaurants were seafood oriented. Artist colonies painted every manner of seascape, sunrise, sunset, and white-capped wave. Catalina Island was the visible yet alluring weekend getaway, and surfing and sailing were the popular sports.

Spring break meant hanging out on the beaches, bicycling the Boardwalk, and gawking at the thousands of inlanders clogging the streets and sun-burning on the sand. The Beach Boys' "California Girls" was on every radio, woody's had surfboards poking out of back windows, and the rich smell of Coppertone permeated the beaches. With jealous seagulls crying and soaring overhead, Newport was an unforgettable sensory experience.

No matter how idyllic our lives were on the southern California coast, children move away and make their own futures in new environments. As the eldest, Harriet married and started a family, first a son, Eric, and then a daughter, Kris. They lived in California, moved to north Idaho, then eventually to the coast of Washington. Along the way, she earned degrees in accounting and law, divorced, and eventually married Lynn, a scientist in marine biology. They have a cabin overlooking Puget Sound, and Harriet, once again, is drawn to the salty sea air and the beautiful rhythm of the tides.

 Louise, truly her father's daughter, never left the Harbor. She graduated with degrees in philosophy and law. Having lived her entire life near the ocean and loving the community, she turned her law background to working in real estate, welcoming newcomers to her beloved Newport Beach. Her stylish fashion and outgoing personality are perfect for her profession, and she and her husband, Craig, thrive being around people, just like our Dad.

Mountains and valleys filled with deer, moose, and elk began to call to Daddy. Mom was ready to try her hand at gardening, so they decided to make their home in northern Idaho. Whether their surroundings were forested or salt-drenched, the two of them were inseparable.

I finished high school early and moved to a town in north Idaho about 30 miles from Mom and Dad. When I enrolled in college I joined the choir, because I enjoyed the friendships and the harmonies. I spent very little time thinking about the religious themes of the music, or the possibility of honestly being labeled a hypocrite. Atheism was making more and more sense to me, but to be fair, I gave religion no opportunity for rebuttal.

Weekends were often spent shooting pool in my parents' basement with the neighboring farm boys. My dad taught me masse shots, bank shots, and how to start with a crisp break. Young eyes helped, and eventually I became a formidable opponent, amateur, but still challenging.

After two years of college, I moved to southern Idaho to earn a four-year degree in elementary education. Just across the street from the football stadium was The Suds, a friendly, smoky, aging beer joint. And I am proud to say the pool table therein paid for most of my college beer drinking, which was copious.

It was high school I hated, not learning, so choosing a career in teaching allowed me to get paid to satisfy my curiosity every day. Life sciences are an integral part of elementary school, and I loved the opportunity to turn kids on to the powers of scientific theories. Sharing the world of nature with my students and enjoying the outdoors with John, my husband, meant my time was filled with personal and professional satisfaction.

For sixteen years of Idaho living, Mom and Dad experienced the snows of winter, the mud of spring, about 20 glorious summer days, and then the snows again. But they loved it. Stark beauty, senses always on alert, and physical and mental challenges. The locals called northern Idaho "God's Country". I heard that and wondered to whom the rest of the country belonged.

Mom welcomed our visits with home-made enchiladas and lemon meringue pies. Daddy worked on our cars and argued with our politics. Their two grandchildren, Harriet's gifts, were their new beneficiaries of intellectual challenges and thought-provoking projects.

Without a Song

I only know there ain't no love at all, without a song

And then suddenly, when she was just 58, Mom's lungs showed the ugly grays of cancer, most likely from those childhood games under the crop duster's spray. Two brothers and her little sister died of lung cancer and emphysema, so her disease was not surprising. But it was so agonizing. Betty and Jim had just celebrated their 40th wedding anniversary. Daddy had cared for her as best he could, but she had always been the one to nurture and heal. He had always made their environment possible for healing to take place.

Friends came by to visit and more than once one would mention how "unfair" it was that she had cancer at such a relatively young age. Her response was stunning. "Fair? Would it be more fair if someone else had this disease?"

When I said I was sorry she was only going to celebrate 40 years of marriage her reply was typical Mom: "I've been happily married to your father for 40 years. Some women don't even have four years of a happy marriage. I am fortunate and very thankful."

One of our favorite songs to sing at family gatherings was The Beatles "When I'm 64". Mom would play the piano and anyone who was around sang along. Even Daddy would join in, stressing the "will you still feed me" lines with gusto. He didn't make it to 64 before Mom passed away.

There were only two times in my life that I saw my father cry. The first was when I told him I had just returned from hitchhiking from Boise to Mexico and back again with a girlfriend, similar to what he had done when he was young. He cried then, and when I asked why, he said "because I was 6'4" tall and a big guy You are just a slip of a little girl, and you're my little girl, and how can I protect you when go and do crazy things like that?" and he then cried even harder.

The second time, we were standing in their kitchen about to go visit Mom in the hospital. The phone rang and I was told by my sister that Mom had just died. When I told my Daddy, my big strong Daddy, he crumpled near the counter and wept.

All I could do was hold him tight and weep with him, two scared souls kneeling on the kitchen floor.

And I inherited my mother's piano.

Mom had asked for a Catholic memorial service to be held at the mortuary. The priest, whom she had never met but who had asked for narrative from others before the service, spoke of her rich life and her generous contributions to her family and community. She had been working for the school district as the nutritionist and had started the first breakfast program for needy children in the state. The district's school cooks loved her and came to her memorial, filling the mortuary with working women, women supporting their families. The pianist played "When Irish Eyes Are Smiling", to no dry eyes.

Mom wanted her ashes to be sprinkled by the mortuary, in the forest, so no one would feel obligated to visit a grave or be tied to a particular area. She did not want to be a bother. Mothers sacrifice in life, and often, even in death.

Jim loved Betty for 40 years, 7 months, and 18 days, plus the three months of 1946 prior to their wedding. When Mom died, Daddy was lost. She was the woman who had offered him a far better life than he would have found on the race track and in the pool halls. And now he was adrift.

He tried living in Baja, California for a few years, fishing the richest sea, soaking in the warmth, and accepting the pace. He enjoyed his Jose Cuervo. "Last Hurrah" was what Dad called his tequila, tonic, and lime. He would have several Last Hurrahs in an evening, because "they help with leg cramps".

He would visit Harriet in Washington, and he tried living in southern Idaho with me and my husband, but southern California eventually lured him back home. Louise had never left Newport, and she lovingly helped him make the transition to a senior community where the sunny days would help him enjoy his time. Dad had visits from his daughters and grandchildren, yet he was alone, without Mom, for 24 years, from age 62.

Newport had, over the course of sixty years, evolved into a resort with thousands of multi-million dollar homes, and hundreds of million dollar boats moored at their private docks. One of Dad's favorite excursions was cruising the harbor in an electric Duffy Boat. Duffy's are basically saltwater golf carts, perfect for scenic strolls at 5 miles per hour, while oohing and aahing and dreaming of luxury. They are not allowed out past the Jetty, but within the harbor, they are wonderful for small group dining and drinking.

On special occasions we would rent a Duffy, sip our wine while Daddy savored his Last Hurrah, and putt through the channels among the islands. We'd always wave at the sign by the Balboa Island Ferry that read "JD's Big Game Tackle". John, or JD as he is now known, worked for our parents at the gun club before he started his tackle business. Daddy would raise his glass of tequila and toast to John's success as an entrepreneur. Having been self-employed, Daddy, without a high school diploma, knew the perseverance it took to be prosperous in such an affluent community.

Our Dad loved the ocean, married a girl of the coast, raised their daughters on the peninsula, and lived with the pulse of the tides. The Navy was in his courage, boats were in his passion, and always, salt water was in his veins. His heart and his hands were wonderfully strong, but his failing lungs finally took our Daddy away. The years of welding and breathing toxic fumes in his muffler business tried to have the final word. Louise refused to allow that, and instead, she held him tight and whispered in his ear "Please give us a sign that you will be ok. We love you, Daddy."

.

Sentimental Journey

Gotta take that sentimental journey,

sentimental journey home

Daddy did not want a church service or graveyard words. He wanted his grandkids, daughters, and sons-in law to have a pleasant and peaceful goodbye. His request was to have his ashes return to the salty currents, to drift out through the Jetty, visit the shores of the Amalfi Coast, and then ride the tides back again past Mother's Beach and return to the arms of his beautiful bay. We would do our part, and then it would be up to the tides and currents to do theirs.

Since Harriet, Louise, and I, along with our spouses Lynn, Craig, and John, and Harriet's two children Eric and Kris, could not get together on the same weekend, nor could we all fit into one Duffy boat, we made plans to honor his wish on two separate occasions. We divided Daddy's ashes into three Chinese take-out containers, and Louise then divided hers · in half, since she would be participating in both memorials.

The first weekend, John and I, Louise and Craig, and Bill, a family friend, rented the little boat. We celebrated Daddy's life, his gifts of curiosity and questioning authority, and his amazing strength of character. We cut the limes, measured the Jose Cuervo, and splashed in the tonic water. We toasted our father drinking this favorite, his Last Hurrah, with tears, laughs, and insecurity.

Louise sprinkled Daddy's ashes throughout our harbor cruise, near his old muffler shop on the bay, just off Mom's Beach, and along the Jetty. I reached over the side and began tipping my container of ashes as we drifted by Mother's Beach, but I could feel another boat pulling along side of us. Not quite certain that putting ashes in Newport's waters was legal, I looked up to see if it was the Harbor Patrol.

With a sigh of relief I continued pouring out my Daddy's ashes. As the passing yacht pulled away, we all were struck by the name on the stern of the yacht. Louise and I began sobbing...with hope and joy. Daddy had indeed given us his "everything is ok" sign. I felt truly blessed. I could never have asked for a greater gift.

In large bold letters it read:

The Last Hurrah

Unchained Melody

God speed your love to me

The following weekend was another opportunity to celebrate and memorialize our Daddy. Harriet, Lynn, Eric, and Kris, along with Louise, Craig, and Bill, rented another Duffy Boat. Being treated equally was always important to us as we were growing up, and in our adulthood, we were still conscious of things being fair. We wanted Daddy's goodbye to be fair for us all.

Louise recounted to me at the end of the day that the cruise was lovely. Louise and I had both told Harriet about the inspiring event of the last weekend; of seeing the Last Hurrah. Harriet is more subdued than we are, so she reserved her explanation for a less emotional time. However, the questions of afterlife, supreme beings, and the dimensions of time and space were rising in the corners of our minds.

On this second weekend, again, everyone was enjoying the celebration of life, sipping their Last Hurrahs, and telling stories of Daddy and Mom's adventures. They talked about being so fortunate to have loving parents and a healthy environment, and wonderful childhoods.

Just as before, Louise sprinkled the last of her share of Daddy's ashes throughout the harbor. As Harriet draped her arm over the side of the boat to begin pouring out her ashes, another boat pulled alongside to pass the slow moving Duffy Boat. Louise said the scene was identical to the week before, with Mother's Beach in the background. Of course, it wasn't the Last Hurrah that was passing their memorial boat. No. It wasn't. It was a sailboat and not a yacht. On the stern of the graceful sailboat was just one word:

Betty

Till the End of Time

the one you love and live for

We have talked about the what-ifs, the blending of space with time, the strength of a soul, the lasting love of a parent for a child, of a woman for a man, and the bonds of sisters. We have no answers. We were raised to fill our lives with questions, so we question still.

Whether it is the hand of a God with which we are unfamiliar, or the dimensions of a science with which our century is unfamiliar, we know with our hearts and minds there is grace. We've seen grace with our own eyes.

We could sit back and enjoy this new-found comfort, this intangible evidence of life after death that brings hope and the tantalizing hint of infinity. We could explore and examine and attempt a hypothesis to prove or disprove the reality of what we experienced.

The fact remains, we felt presence with the boats; we saw written language with words that hold special meaning. This grace was not subtle — it was cutting through the sea beside us. Their undying love for each other was also the gift of parental love for us. Till the end of time.

∞∞

Hearts

&

Minds

The Pacific Coast Highway

Newport Beach, California, circa 1956
as seen through the eyes of a four year old

Standing with my back against a brick building, a locked door on one side and a parking lot on the other, I watched the cars speeding by. Some were slowing to stop for the traffic light down the block, while others were speeding up trying to make up for lost time. A few shoppers were walking on the sidewalk on the opposite side of PCH, and every once in awhile someone would jaywalk from one side to the other when the traffic allowed.

Mostly though, it was cars whirring by, exhaust fumes clinging to the breeze. Many people looked at me from their passenger windows, but no one stopped. No one walked by me on my side of the street. I was standing in front of my daddy's muffler shop, but not a lot of people go window shopping for tailpipes in this beach town.

I didn't like standing there. The sidewalk looked dirty and hard and had old gum stuck on it, so sitting was not an option. Besides, I was wearing my favorite plaid dress with the white Peter Pan collar and a fluffy new slip. My slip would get yucky if I sat down. So I stood, balancing first on one foot, then on the other, shifting my little weight as the minutes dragged on and on.

Louise and Harriet, my two older sisters, were in school on this day, but I was too young for kindergarten, so I was standing under the big white sign with red letters shouting JIM'S MUFFLER SERVICE.

Daddy had to drive to Huntington Beach to return a car he had worked on, so Mom and I drove her car to the shop, and then we would follow him to Huntington Beach. Daddy would drop off the customer's car, get in our car, and Mom would give him a ride back to the shop.

Huntington Beach is just north of Newport Beach a few miles, straight up the coast on the PCH. Being only four, I didn't know how far away Huntington was, but I knew that I would get to go for a ride along the ocean. I didn't know if I was going to be riding in our car with my mom, or the customer's car with my daddy, but I didn't care. I could roll down the window and listen to the seagulls and catch glimpses of the surfers from either car's back seat. But here I was, still standing under JIM'S MUFFLER SERVICE.

After Daddy locked the front door to the building from the inside, he went out the back door, got in the customer's car, and drove off up the highway. I guessed I was supposed to wait by the front door for my mom so I could ride in our own car. So, I waited. And waited.

Four years old on a busy highway with strangers all around. I knew something was wrong. Mom never came to get me. She never pulled by me in the parking lot and said "hop in". I thought she would, so I kept a close eye on the lot we had parked in. But our car wasn't there, my mom wasn't there, the door was locked, and Daddy had left long ago. I tried to make plaid blend into the bricks.

It wasn't so much that I was scared. It was more that I was worried. I worried that my parents might not miss me. Or maybe they wouldn't miss me until I wasn't sitting in my spot at the dinner table. Or maybe I should have started walking in the direction that I thought they drove. Maybe they would be mad that I didn't try to find them.

I didn't know if I was doing anything wrong, but I also didn't think standing idle was doing anything right, either. How could I do the right thing if I didn't know what it was? I wanted to be a good girl, but what do good girls do when all they see are strange cars going by with their exhaust stinking up the air at just the right height of a four year old? It was noisy, smelly, and my feet hurt from standing in one place.

I waited for a long time. I didn't cry, but I swallowed a lot. Would I be in trouble? It wasn't what I had done; it was what I hadn't done. I hadn't gotten into a car. I wasn't riding with my mom or my dad. I wanted to mind, but I didn't know what minding looked like on the PCH. So, I smashed my back into that brick wall, shifted from left foot to right foot, and worried, heart sinking.

What would I do if a stranger came by? I shouldn't ask for help because I wasn't supposed to talk to strangers. But everybody was a stranger on this highway, so who could I ask? It might be better to just be small and quiet against the wall. Maybe Daddy would spot me when he came to work the next day.

But my feet were really hurting and I wanted to sit down so badly. There was sand on the sidewalk and ants wandering around in the cracks and if I sat down they might get into my panties. Louise said when I wiggled too much that I "had ants in my pants," and I knew I didn't want that.

As an adult, I know the distance between my brick building and downtown Hunting Beach was about 6 miles. In Newport traffic, and a few signal lights, the one-way trip might take about 20 minutes. Mom made it to the city limits of Huntington Beach before she spotted my dad's customer's car. She said she kept looking to see my head above the back of the seat, but she couldn't see me. Finally, she signaled him to pull over; they figured out that neither had their youngest daughter as a passenger, and Mom drove like "a bat out of hell" back to the Muffler Shop.

And there I was. For forty minutes my 40 or so pounds had been holding up the front of the building, waiting, waiting for a smiling face. And then finally, there was my mom, her face all streaky and red, sniffling and panting. She held me so close I could feel her heart thumping through her chest, right there on the sidewalk. She didn't say anything, she just held me tight. Maybe I was in trouble. No words were not comforting words.

I blurted out through my tears that I was sorry, that I didn't know what I was supposed to do, and that I just stood there by the door. Mom finally held me out at arms' length and looked me in the eyes. When she caught her breath, she told me I did just the right thing. That nobody could have been any smarter or braver.

I was so relieved, but also puzzled by her words because I hadn't known what to do and so I hadn't done anything at all. Smart knows what to do, and I didn't. Brave does something like a hero, so how could doing nothing be brave? When you are little and you are worried and you are alone, you don't feel very smart or very brave at all.

****

I wasn't standing on the Pacific Coast Highway all that long in adult minutes, but in children's minutes, it was forever. It was the certainty of being vulnerable and the uncertainty of wise choices. Others' actions and our responses have roots which we don't even remember, yet those roots have been tangling in our psyches for a lifetime.

As the years passed, I realized I had become wary of locking doors, uncertain of my role in situations requiring shuttles, and exacting in logistics. These behaviors are quirky, but not overtly controlling nor debilitating. However, the intense anxiety of waiting for someone and the self-doubt of not being in the correct place at the correct time is ongoing, even 58 years later, and requires immense restraint to avoid panic.

Parenting is so challenging and childhood is so malleable. If being forgotten on a sidewalk can carve such lasting and deep fears, what other circumstances and behaviors are quietly gripping the lives of our children, leaving them alone and standing silently, against a wall.

∞∞

Cross My Heart

She was warm, gentle, tentative—

a curious frightened child, vulnerable.

I was towering tall, imposing—

her new teacher, a stranger.

Our morning read aloud, *Amos and Boris*

Was a story of heartfelt friendship.

With students on the floor surrounding my chair,

Mary, on her first day in our class,

chose to kneel at my side.

She tugged on my skirt's hem

with strawberry jam on every finger.

Her eyes took in my laugh lines,

and frown lines,

and glances even remotely her way.

My eyes took in haunting desperation

bedraggled,

no braids, no bows.

The rolling rhythm of the tale—

whispered secrets, stormy tirades,

and then the calm of resolution.

The story wove my voice into her heart.

So trusting was she.

We both have much to give,

but she had much more to lose.

Faith in me, a chance for pride in herself.

If I were to fail her—

speak sharply, glare angrily, move brusquely...

Learning with me would not be possible,

if I harmed those tenuous ties.

When the story was over, I tried to rise,

But her grubby, chubby fingers

now trembled around my waist.

Acceptance or rejection—

Mary waited anxiously for a sign.

Would I hold her and hug her?

Her sticky jam...her smudge?

Or would I gently but irrevocably

push her aside—alone, ashamed.

In just a thirty-minute time

this child was mine.

Waiting, hopeful, cautious—

hinging on my mood,

on my temperament,

hinging on my heart.

∞ ∞

Perch Surprise

Can I take her heart home and show my Mom?

Life science, and biology in particular, is exciting to teach to young children. They are eager to learn about animals, their insides and their outsides, what they eat and how they poop, and can they be petted. Especially can they be petted. Touch is the ultimate instructor.

In Idaho, in the winter under the ice of the frozen Cascade Reservoir, perch fish are often quite plentiful. Since they are not a game fish, there is no limit to the number of perch that can be caught and kept. Some are quite large, but in many years they are about 6-8 inches long. Fresh out of the water, perch are a striking gold with black stripes and sharp points on the dorsal fin.

Every year for about fifteen years, my husband, John, and I went ice fishing to catch enough perch so my second/third grade students could each have their own fish to dissect. We'd catch the perch on worms, take them home whole, and freeze them. Then, on the day of the dissection, I'd thaw the fish so they were ready to cut into by early afternoon. No one wants to dissect a fish right before lunch.

On the day prior to the dissection, the students were shown a diagram of the perch labeling each of the fins, the gills, the eyes, the anus, and the mouth. Learning the word "anus" was extremely exciting. They knew that the surgeon scientist would use scissors to gently poke into the anus, snip up the belly to just below the jaw, and then snip toward the gills, exposing like an open window all the fantastic parts within.

One parent volunteer would oversee every two students. I asked the kids before dissection day who wanted to be the scientist that cut the fish open, and who wanted to be the scientist that held the fish steady. No one would be forced to touch a fish, but everyone was encouraged to at least touch one scale.

On the day of the perch dissection, everyone was excited, anxious, and very wiggly, including me. The students were paired based on their stated preference from the day before, and assigned a parent. They were each issued a pair of stubby school scissors and an ice-pick type probe.

Before anyone even received their first perch, I gave a stern lecture about respecting the fish. We were not to disrespect the once living being; we were to learn about the form and function of its body parts. The scissors and probe were tools, not toys. We were scientists, and scientists' work is serious. Parents were to try very hard to coach and not touch. They were there to encourage, but not do the actual cutting.

We would start out with one fish for every two kids. The fish didn't smell (yet) because they were still partially frozen, but they were a little slimy. One of our goals was to have students find and remove the stomach (which often held a worm or two), the intestines (which often held "fishpoop"), the gills, the heart, and maybe, an egg sac.

The egg sac was always fascinating. Out of 24 perch, usually only one or two are male. The egg sac holds about 50,000 eggs, if I remember correctly, and is shaped like a small Twinkie, in a lovely peach color. "Mine's a girl!" and "Oooh, mine is too!" rang repeatedly throughout the room. Female fish were hungrier than males in mid-winter, and theories were proposed as to why. "Feeding eggs" was a popular conclusion for these young biologists.

Interestingly, the kids who thought they were only going to help steady the fish always became engrossed in the project and were soon helping to probe and snip to the point where no one remembered who was the "surgeon scientist" and who was the "holder scientist". Squeemish was totally gone as soon as cool fish parts started being shown from desk to desk. A few times, it was the parent who had to sit back and take a deep breath, but the kids were diving in and amazed.

As students were finishing up the first fish, it was time to surprise them with one more dissection. I hadn't told them about it because it is difficult to imagine if you haven't already gotten your fingers entwined in intestines or held the perfectly shaped little heart.

"We're going to look for little crystal balls, tiny, clear, and clean, and there are two of them in each fish. They are smaller than a freckle and bigger than a pencil dot." Anticipation was palpable, even with the parents. "We are going to look inside the fish's eyes to find these crystal balls." "Ewwww."

After a short discussion about how far we've all come as scientists, the kids were ready to find the crystal balls. We took out the fish eyes, cut them open and discovered the lens within. If you gently hold a fish lens over a letter printed on a newspaper, the lens magnifies the letter. (Fish-eye camera comes to mind.)

Interestingly, the lenses from the same perch were often different sizes. Again, theories abounded.

"Maybe they are nearsighted?" Try to imagine 24 kids and 12 parents peering into fish eyes and spotting a tiny clear ball in all that fluid and tissue, and no one is grossed out. Science is so exciting!

Finishing up with the eyes and seeing an opening in the fish's head, it was obvious we needed to locate the fish's brain, so snip and poke we did. Suddenly, the tiniest gray blob, shocking that it could control the perch's every movement, was being walked around the room in some child's palm, showing everyone what a fantastic brain surgeon she was going to be someday. Soon, everyone was excitedly saying, "I found a brain, too!"

Then it was time for the second fish, and by this time everyone was an experienced "surgeon scientist". The second fish was dissected, and now-familiar body parts and their functions were analyzed and reported on. Each child wanted to take home what he/she had found and show parents and siblings, so plastic bags were handed out and promptly filled up with glorious fish parts. The lovely lenses got their own little baggie with a touch of water to keep them moist.

Oddly, other students from other classes would walk by our room and hold their noses. My kids thought that was hilarious. They realized they had gotten used to the smell as the fish thawed, and didn't know their fish had stunk up the building.

Science doesn't always smell like roses, as parents discovered later that evening when open Ziplocks of fish organs were displayed on their dinner tables. Whatever the smell, these kids learned a lot about themselves from these little perch, not the least of which was personal courage.

How Dare The Man Quit Life

a friend lost

Such depths of despair are the height of ingratitude.

But then, perhaps he knew not sanity.

That is the only sane explanation.

That must be how he dared.

I could never kill myself

as long as there are flannel sheets in the white of a winter
night,

or strawberries are in season, or if a turkey might gobble,

or salmon are running, or when winds are in pines,

somewhere.

I couldn't quit

before the crocus bloomed, or the last tomato ripened,

or the fire-orange sunsets ceased to be.

I might give up and end it all

when an upside-down duck doesn't make me giggle,

and avocados aren't creamy on my tongue,

and ice on the trees doesn't sparkle like my mother's

beaded purse,

and when brown-eyed beagles don't melt my heart....

all on the same Saturday at noon.

But until that day,

get out of my way.

There are songbirds in the dawn,

crunches in my cereal,

and coconuts in my shampoo.

I have soft t-shirts with long enough sleeves,

hot red polish on my toenails,

and my jeans are not too tight.

There is the river to float, the creek to wade,

the ocean to smell, the lake to fish.

There is the forest to hear, the desert to search,

the mountain to climb, the park to walk.

There is the library to think, the music to dance,

the ball game to shout, the zoo to awe.

There is, above all else, the man who loves me, to love.

There is far too much texture left to be felt to stop touching

too soon.

The shallow thought, the narrow scope, the dearth of

curiosity is baffling.

To be unmoved and uncaring about this wondrous life
defies reason to the healthy of mind and body.

For the hurting, the confused, the mercurial, the multiple,
through genetic predisposition or environmental trauma,
we do not yet have definitive cures or even answers.

We still have pain and personal confusion and questions,
and people willing, perhaps eager, to quit.

I want to go when the last worm has turned over the last
bit of soil and all that remains is a desolate crust of Earth.

Then I will go quietly.
And I will be grateful
for my sanity.

∞ ∞

On The Banks of the Boise River

Goslings were born
on the banks of the Boise.

They were scrawny and ugly.
Learning to swim the current
--when to drift, when to fight—
They grew stronger.

They were demanding and hungry.
Offered tidbits and banquets,
Scrabbling for savory morsels
served at a riverside feast.

They grew stronger.

Goose, gander; all strutted, preened.

Goose, gander; all protective, nurturing.

Wings first akimbo, but then interlaced

they protected the sanctity

of their community.

They too were hungry and demanding.

They too grew stronger.

First flight—awkward, gangly.

Goslings with damp flight feathers

began to carom off the cottonwoods.

Gentle coaxing, firm coaching,

brought tentative freedom

then brash exhilaration.

They grew stronger.

Knowing they wanted to go,

but not knowing why—

Knowing they were leaving,

but not knowing for where—

The maturing goslings trusted,

and followed.

To catch the wind

To strive to keep up

To rest in another's wake

To be so bold as to share the lead,

They each grew stronger.

This small V honked

echoing, proudly echoing,

learners and teachers triumphant.

They took to the sky,

a lesson in endurance

they will experience together.

They've gone miles—

They have miles, and mountains yet to go.

When the geese come back—

for they will be geese,

and they will come back-

it will be to nurture and protect,

coax and coach,

preen, and strut,

and teach.

And we will all grow stronger.

A poem, for Lamont Lyons , gander

and Phyllis Edmundson, goose

Professors, Curriculum and Instruction

 1st Doctoral Graduation 1997

Boise State University

by Eileen, one of 10 goslings

∞ ∞

Don't Tell Anyone, But…

When Mrs. Malone came to help paint clay pots for art,

her daughter's second grade classmates were forewarned

that Mrs. Malone had "eaten bean burritos for dinner last night

and farted all through breakfast ruining everyone's Cheerios."

****

Despite the fact that deer season wasn't yet open,

Rick informed the class his Dad shot a deer in the forest over the weekend

and it was now hanging in the garage where their old truck used to be parked.

Something as fascinating as a furry, four-legged bleeding body

dangling next to the clothes dryer from its antlers has got to be shared.

****

Amy quietly borrowed Freddy, one of the class frogs, to show her new baby brother.

She put it in her pocket before recess at 10:00 and forgot to take it out at home at 4:00.

Mom found Freddy after the jeans were washed, and Sue and Amy are no longer best friends.

There is no way that tragedy was going to be kept a secret in the second grade.

****

"Scooter's humping Barney and they're both boys!" Cassie loudly announced.

And indeed, he was and they were, and now all wide eyes were upon them.

They were lop-ear rabbits who just happened to be getting it on as vigorously as they could, under a student's desk.

I didn't recall Professor Hill's Curriculum and Instruction class ever addressing the proper way to discuss fornicating bisexual lagomorphs, and particularly not with nine-year old children in a public school setting.

"OK, class, let's get out our spelling books" was not going to cut it.

"This will be our little secret" wouldn't make it past first recess.

Time to encourage parental involvement. "Please talk about this relationship with your parents tonight." /grin.

****

Teachers should get medals for discretion in the face of innocent humor, and compassion in the face of crushing reality:

A second grader is wielding a pair of handcuffs that she lifted off of the headboard in her parents' bedroom and is now sharing with the class.

* *

Two seven-year-old boys were waging war in the backpack storage area by shooting a pair of rolled-in-removal adult black lace panties like a giant rubberband. No one claimed to have brought them.

* *

A young boy being given a ride home from school has to knock on his neighbors' door. He isn't allowed to knock on the door of his own home "because Mom might have clients".

∞ ∞

Why I Love Willie

Willie's momma was a whore

   I know, 'cause Willie told me so.

His daddy drove a bright yellow Cadillac

   I know, 'cause I saw him driving with the top down.

In Boise, Idaho, you sort of notice those things.

Willie cried when Ben called him a nigger

I know, 'cause my blouse was soaked with his pain.

His Grandpa thought Willie was a joyous treasure

Willie knows how to whittle.

In elementary school, you sort of notice those things.

Willie and I taught Willie to read

Lord knows, no one at home could.

Willie loved learning and laughing

He giggled every time he read *The Walking Coat*.

In third grade, you sort of notice those things.

Willie moved on to another state, another city, again

One warm black face gone from our sea of white

One tender soul,

One scared boy,

One whittler,

Gone.

Our little community has an empty ache

where Willie's laughter once was.

In a teacher's heart, you sort of notice those things.

∞ ∞

Boobs

or

Not

Boobs

Anxiety from Age Three

My mother had big boobs. Two of them. I had two sisters, Harriet and Louise. If one boob fed Harriet, and the other fed Louise, who fed me? I was three and I could count, and obviously there were not enough boobs to share equally. Being the youngest, I knew someone else had to either be my mother or someone loaned her an unwanted boob. I didn't like either reality.

When a child can hold up the correct number of fingers for her age, you can bet she can count boobs. I was devastated. This woman who claimed to be my mother must not have held me close to her heart like she did with my older sisters. They each must have drunk all the milk in their respective boobs, leaving nary a boob with Mother's Milk in it for me. So who fed me? And if my mom didn't nurse me, did she still hold me close and cuddle me? Boobs, or the lack thereof, tormented me. Little did I know the worst was yet to come.

When I was nine years old, Harriet, at 13, decided to grow these gigantic shapely knockers. Sure, she was modest and discreet, but there is no hiding 36 DD tits on a tall red head. Of course, Mom had to take her to special bra stores so the straps wouldn't cut into her shoulders. And don't forget the underwires and the heart crossers for a girl so fortunately endowed. Yeah, yeah, yeah. "Leenie, your turn will come. Just be patient." Yeah, yeah, yeah.

When I was eleven years old, Louise, at 13, developed delicate, tasteful breasts; not too big, not too small, not too pointy, not too droopy. Just totally fashionable globes of perfection. She sewed Audrey Hepburn silk blouses that clung to her curves and accentuated creamy olive skin with subtle hints of the cleavage that lay demurely beneath the lapels. And yeah, yeah, yeah. "Leenie, just wait. You'll be next." Yeah, yeah, yeah.

So, I turned 13. "OK, I'm waiting." fingers tap tap tap. "ok, any time now" tap tap tap. Nothing. Nada. Zilch. Mom took me to Penney's to buy a Littlest Angel Starter Bra, a AAA elastic harness which was supposed to preclude momentous physiological outheaval. tap tap tap.

I had already started my period, I had already sprouted the requisite zits, I had already learned to flip my hair in contempt, but where were those promised protuberances? Tears of embarrassment and shame and disappointment do not help one's complexion.

My best friend, Vicki, was about five feet tall. She had breasts that stuck two feet out in front of her. Her mom so cleverly said, "I can always tell when Vicki is entering the room because her breasts poke through the doorway first". Yeah, right, and thanks a lot for that information.

But Vicki was smart enough to not tell me she had to go to the Bali Bras store to get those shoulder-savers with the metal trusses that could support a highway bridge. Vicki was thrilled, but also reserved and quiet. But it wasn't enough. Her boobs played a HUGE role in the demise of our teenage friendship.

Penny, a non-friend in sixth grade, had breasts so big she had to use a sweater chain to keep her cardigans closed because the buttons weren't stout enough to do the required heavy lifting. And in junior high, Penny could never find her freaking towel while naked in the shower room. Boingg, boingg. "Have you seen my blue towel?" Boingg boingg. "Maybe it's over here." Boingg boingg.

Bra Fraud

Two years of being encumbered and hoodwinked by the Littlest Angel were enough for me. The only time my body pretended it was a budding young woman was when it was cold. Cute little nipples would jut out like miniature islands on a vast calm ocean. What a cruel quirky side Mother Nature was showing.

Sixteen years old and then, horror of horrors, puny and pointy boobies decided to grow. Now grow is a relative term. From a Triple A to a Double A is not something to write home about. These little TaTas did not require containment. My mom finally reached the conclusion that perhaps I wouldn't be developing real breasts any time this lifetime. Her helpful response when I pleaded with her for some optimism: "Well, at least you won't have to spend a fortune on bras".

And that was finally the truth. Why on earth would any sane woman choose to bind herself into such a contraption if she had nothing to put in it? I gave up worrying about my nipples poking out and I gave up hope for any measureable amount of breast tissue. Fortunately for me, at the same time reality struck, so did feminism, and bras were tossed out of style for many a brazen woman.

Boys and Bikinis

Speaking of reality, when a girl is flat-chested, she knows her boyfriends aren't showing her off on the town for her beautiful body. She knows her dates aren't eager to get her undressed, well the top half, anyway. There is a sense of resignation and acceptance when a girl matures and other qualities besides bras size (perhaps the joy of existence?) become important.

I came to accept the fact, albeit kicking and screaming, that Harriet inherited our mother's breasts, Louise inherited our Aunt Pat's breasts, and I inherited our father's chest. It is what it is, or in this case, it is what it isn't.

Shopping for bikinis was always humiliating. In southern California it is mandated that teenage citizens parade about on the Boardwalk and bicycle and skateboard in their bathing attire. Skinny, titless, and freckled, I tried to do my part. It was hell. But there is no better environment than the Pacific's beaches to learn to shrug and move on. Resigned acceptance gave way to nonchalance. Humor and time won.

From Flat to Flatter

From forty years of age on, I diligently withstood the mortification of attempts at mammograms. The technicians were always professional and apologetic, and they did their best to secure x-rays of non-compliant boobies. I tried to jolly them along so they would not pity me, and most appreciated that my joking manner helped them through their task.

And then, at the age of 54, a technician discovered a lump. That lump was equivalent to about 50% of my left breast, even though it was a very tiny lump. I had felt it, but thought nothing of it. There was no history of breast cancer in my family, and I figured that without much breast, what are the odds of actually having cancer? Wrong, wrong. The words every woman, whether flat, buxom, skinny, or soft, is petrified of hearing: "You have cancer."

At home, John and I talked about my fears, anger, and betrayal. We talked about what the future might hold. Then, after hearing options from the oncologist and surgeon, my decision was fast, firm, and confident.

Whack. And I might as well whack off both, because one of these little tas isn't going to look all that appealing under a t-shirt, not that they ever had as a duo. And why risk getting cancer in the neighboring breast? What irony. Grow up without the satisfaction of a seductive body, only to have those miserable wannabes turn traitor and get cancerous. How does one react with equanimity when once again, Mother Nature betrays one of her own gender. Talk about bad juju.

The surgeon asked if I wanted to have reconstruction, because if I did, she would save some of the surrounding skin to use in the rebuilding. Now wouldn't you think that someone who had been perfectly flat would jump at the chance to instantly become Dolly Partonish? or even a Mia Farrow twin? Nope.

I had learned to live with this un-voluptuous body. What would be the point of going into old age with monster jugs. I had fantasized about having a gorgeous set throughout my childhood and teenage years. That was then. Get real. I would have to wear *a bra*. I asked the surgeon if she had a model that I could pump up when I went out to a fancy dinner and then I could let the air out when I went bouncing cross-country on my ATV. She said no, so I said no.

And a Toast to Women, With and Without Boobs

I do miss not having responsive nipples. But that is the extent of my dismay. I had never had breast augmentation because by the time I could afford it, I realized it was only the men looking at me that would appreciate their appearance. I don't stare at my chest. Why would I go through surgery and recovery for strangers? My husband didn't need boobs to love me in the first place.

I had already had two open-heart surgeries as a five-year-old. The repair of congenital heart defects in the 1950's had left my chest scarred from armpit to armpit. As a freshman at North Idaho College, a shockproof Green Beret with whom I was going skinny-dipping was stunned. "Jesus Christ! It looks like someone took off after you with an axe!" Now if that doesn't make a young woman self-conscious, nothing will.

Remember my friend Vicki with the very enviable knockers? Years later, I gave up blaming her for my flat chest and we took up our friendship where we had left off. When I went through chemo she told me that she would have had hers cut off, too, if she were diagnosed with cancer. She said having boobs, though, *is* a lot of fun. Right after I slugged her, we both agreed that breathing was more important.

Reaching that "ah hah" state took introspection. John has always recognized and defended the concept that women are more than bodies. His disdain for the shallow vanity promoted by advertisers and Hollywood is what gave me the confidence to push my shoulders back and stand tall. If I couldn't strut an appearance rich with stunning desire, I could choose to be dignified.

Coming to terms with who I am, what makes me the woman I am, follows the same path every woman travels. We have to look deeply, beyond the boobs, and live for the fun of it. We deserve, and demand, to be recognized as valuable contributors to our world.

Whether we have giant melons or miniscule titties or even no breasts at all, women are capable, successful, and worthy of lovers with whom we choose to laugh and live. We are not our boobs.

∞ ∞

Chemo,

Let Me Count the Ways

It was hell, flirting with heaven..

It was sickening and weakening,

it was stoic and strengthening,

it was poison.

I thankfully hate it with all my heart.

The power to spew out your guts

and crush in your brain.

The power to ulcerate your skin

and devastate your hair.

The power to numb your memory

and steal your courage.

Minutes, hours, days, weeks, months,

and then the blessed End.

A new, used you.

Frightened, heroic.

At sea on land, alone, confused,

yet almost ready to smile.

Time is the gift, the healer, the hope,

And survivors are forever wondering

how long forever will be.

∞ ∞

The Orchid Cloche

A gift so surprisingly wonderful,

hopeful, heartfelt, and cherished

"You are bald, as I once was.

Here. A hat I made for you, in a soothing shade.

It will look lovely without the hair you don't have."

Mary Kathryn said these words in a whisper filled with

wisdom, the wisdom of ten years of cancer-free living.

"Your arms, tucked as a wounded bird with shattered

wings, like mine once were.

Come. Reach with me, reach for the sun.

One day, someday, you will breathe deep,

stretch high, and smile."

She said these words patiently, again and again,

knowing my pain of post-mastectomy movement.

"A survivor never forgets.
The little knit hat will help
with the frozen fear that grips your heart.
It will remind you that you are not alone
and that you, too, shall survive."

My orchid cloche was warm in December,
and soft when I needed soft.
It was fragile and delicate when I was.
It felt feminine, when I wasn't
and so desperately wanted to be.

Now it adorns the top of my mirror.
I breathe, stretch, and smile.
I smile at this reflection,
a beautiful woman, this woman with curls,
who is thankful and reaching high
for the orchid cloche.

∞ ∞

Double D Bra Gap Blitz

Some schools allow alcohol sales in their stadium. Boise State University doesn't. The vendors charge three dollars for a bottle of water, so I can only imagine what they would charge to spice it up with some Jack, Jim, or BV. A few fans have mentioned they prefer the stadium to be alcohol-free, especially since it is readily available in Tailgate City. My motto is a quote from Maya Angelou: "If you don't like something, change it. If you can't change it, change the way you think about it." So I decided to change it, for one football season, anyway.

After a bilateral mastectomy and chemo, a lady gets thirsty, and exceedingly flat chested. I bought a 38 Double D underwire bra in Tantalizing Teal because it didn't come in Blaze Orange or Bronco Blue.

When my husband saw my purchase he said, "What are *you* gonna do with *that*?" The KitchenAid and I blended up some Cuervo Gold margaritas with lots of crushed ice. I gave the bra a test drive at home, with a shocked look and then a thumbs up from my husband (who wisely listens to BSU games at home on the radio).

****

At the first game, I learned Lesson 1 in chemistry. Ice is cold, it melts, and liquid seeks the lowest level, even when enclosed in a quart Ziplock. A double D holds a full quart of margarita in each cup.

From the parking lot to the security gate, I could feel gravity working on my Jose's. Being a tall woman, rather large breasts did not look out of place, and since I'm no longer 18, having them starting to seriously sag was not unusual either. By the time my friends (two very modest and discreet ladies) and I reached the second level of the stands, there was potential for tragedy. The baggies were blitzing my bellybutton.

I rushed into the restroom and relieved the teal tankards of their cargo. The underwire bra defense was no match for the Ziplock's offense, and the slippage was serious. Too close for comfort, and that also goes for crushed ice next to the chest wall.

After tucking the plastic bags into my purse, I asked for empty drink cups from a vendor. From the uncomfort of our metal bench seats, we sipped our 'ritas, keeping an eye out for burly men in chartreuse neon vests. My wardrobe malfunction required intense intervention if we were going to be ready for next week's game.

****

The second game went better. Yes, the Broncos won the first game, but I was frostbitten. For this game, I used a t-shirt with the words "Brick by Brick" emblazoned on the front as the insulating foundation, then the bra with the cocktails, and then another t-shirt as a shooter.

I also filled some snacksize Ziplocks with trailmix and put those next to the underwire, filling up the gap betwixt body and bra (Yes, gap. The chest wall is actually concave before it rises to meet the sternum.) By putting in the bulky trailmix first, the margarita boobs stayed put, jiggling obscenely against their Nuts & Raisins bulkhead. This top t-shirt was orange and drooped the word "Reload" in blue, low across my chest. Who says engineering isn't fun?

****

As fall drew colder, Bailey's Irish Crème in the mini bottles supplanted the margaritas. A true improvement would be if Baileys started marketing mini-bota-bags of Irish Crème, because the plastic mini-bottles are painful. Delicious and they don't slump, but painful. And please, no hugs.

That whole season was a blast for these three oldladybroncos because not only was our team winning, but every "It's Another Bronco….First Down!" and subsequent touchdown deserved a toast. "To Life! Go Broncos! Go Dougie!"

****

Now I am not advocating breaking the rules and regulations of a football stadium. What I did was Wrong, don't get me wrong. As a social experiment, it was a success, even though no old geezers hustled me, and the studly young gate guards saw no reason to frisk me.

We had fun, and forbidden fruit truly is ever so much better. But when we heard how much the fine would be for getting caught with devil drink in the stadium, we've been dry ever since…well sorta kinda. (And if BSU Security is reading this, we sit in the visitor's section, 2nd level.)

∞ ∞

Thirteen Nipples

Nature is so amazing. We were enjoying the company of Lucy and Bart in our second grade classroom. Lucy was a lovely white rat and Bart was a handsome three-tone black/brown/white rat. They were both friendly with my students and very friendly with each other.

When it became obvious that Lucy was pregnant, we started having class discussions about some of the characteristics of mammals: live birth, mother's milk, four chambered heart, and fur. Our talks were honest and informative, for the students and for me. I am one of the many avid learners when the topic is science, especially a life science.

One afternoon Lucy decided to stretch high on the side of her cage. Rick, a sociable precocious eight year old, clearly proclaimed "Lucy has eight nipples." Several kids rushed over to verify his findings. "Yep. Eight nipples." And then a little worry set in.

Several students wanted to adopt one of Lucy's babies. The kids decided the only fair way to give them away was to have a lottery. Only kids who had a written letter from their parents could put their name in the hat. Once the baby rats were born and thriving, we would draw names out of the hat and those lucky students would have their parents come to school with a brand new cage and drive the little rat and proud rat owner home.

Because there is always potential for classroom pets not surviving, we talked about Lucy's diet and how to keep her healthy. We talked about what she needed to be able to feed her little mammal babies. And we talked about her eight nipples.

Everyone was comfortable with the idea of Lucy having eight babies and being able to nurse them all fairly. But then Christa piped up with "When Mrs. Boots had nine kitties my Daddy said one of them would be a runt!"

"Mrs. Thornburgh, are we going to have a runt?"

Dilemma: How to talk about reproduction when elementary teachers aren't supposed to talk about reproduction. My rationale: we were talking about nurturing the almost born, birth, and hopefully, nourishing the newly born. We wanted Lucy and her babies to be healthy and all equally loved.

We had already kicked Bart out of the family cage for safety's sake. Jeremy had been reading about mouse behavior and pointed out that Daddy mice are not always friendly to baby mice. We decided to err on the safe side with our rats. Bart warranted a cage of his own. I'm certain he and Lucy were both much happier.

We knew Lucy might have only one baby, since this was her first litter. But we also knew she might have eight, or even more. It was the "even more" that was causing the worry. "If Lucy has only eight nipples, how will she feed any extras?" asked Carrie, speaking for virtually everyone.

I recalled my own anxiety as the third child, and wondered if Carrie's mom had talked with her about nursing children. Carrie had younger sisters, so it seemed likely that she had, but still, the numerical incongruity was worrisome for her, as it was for the entire class, including me.

My concern was the very real possibility of having to explain nature's survival of the fittest approach. If Lucy had any babies that weren't healthy or strong, we would be dealing with death and burials rather than new cages with shiny wheels and water bottles. I really didn't want to go there.

Daily discussions centered around Lucy's diet, exercise, and upcoming delivery date.

"I think Lucy needs more fiber."

"Lucy isn't on her wheel as much as before. She'll get too fat!"

"She's so bulgy she looks like she's having waaaay more than eight babies."

"Shouldn't she have popped by now?"

My response to the last question: "Popped? Let's show a little respect for her condition, Tony. How might you pose that question better?"

"Shouldn't she have had births by now?" he quietly offered. Close enough.

Finally, one Monday morning we were greeted by Lucy refusing to come out of her milk carton bedroom. The milk carton had been cut open so the roof was removable, but still provided privacy. For a while we were afraid Lucy would chew her house down, but then she stopped gnawing on it.

Mark's observation, "Wax is yucky when it gets stuck in your teeth. I used to eat my birthday candles when I was little and the red ones left gross hunks of wax. She probably didn't like it, either" had a surprising number of heads bobbing up and down in agreement.

"We gotta be quiet. Babies like quiet" was the rather loud pronouncement made by one student with a brand new baby brother. And our classroom experienced glorious whispering for at least two hours. When it was time for recess, they tip-toed to the outside door and then bolted for the playground to share their fantastic news.

For about three days we heard squeaks and rustling coming from inside the cardboard bedroom. Then curiosity overcame self-discipline and we drew names to see which two kids got the honor of peeking under the carton's roof. The two peepers had to promise not to be noisy near the cage, and they could only count with their eyes, not with their fingers.

"Mrs. Thornburgh! Oh my gosh. There must be ten babies in there! Maybe only nine, but I think ten!"

"I counted eleven, but they were kinda all pink and piled up so maybe not really eleven."

They put the roof back and the excitement was contagious. Maybe eleven babies! "How is she going to feed them all? Should we feed them with an eye dropper like they do the baby kangaroos on *Animal Planet*?"

A few more days passed and Lucy was looking a little thin, but she had a good appetite. Kids brought her extra carrots, chunks of apple, and a broken doggie biscuit to clean her teeth. The noises in the milk carton became more enticing.

I removed the roof and the students filed by, peaking into Lucy's nursery. They were so respectful and patient to Lucy and with each other. I was impressed by their self-control.

The heap of pink babies was also impressive. They were wiggly, squeaky, and demanding. And every one of them was chubby. Quite chubby, actually. For the next few days, with the roof off, we watched the little rats get fuzzier and fatter. Nary a one looked runtish, as was repeatedly pointed out.

Finally, Jeremy's book *Caring for Your Mouse* by Lupo, said we could touch the babies. The time had come for actual hands-on math. And what a shock.

Thirteen baby rats! Lucy had thirteen babies! And each one was thriving. How could this be? Not that I was disappointed. No, I now knew, thankfully, I did not have to worry about death discussions. But what gives with thirteen chubby babies? It was a puzzle for this city-girl teacher and her eager students.

One afternoon Lucy needed a good stretch, a time out from her motherly duties. She climbed on the side of her cage and stretched up as tall as she could, her belly exposed to a couple of smiling faces that were supposed to be reading their chapter books.

The two kids rushed up to me and whispered, "Mrs. Thornburgh! You're not going to believe this! Lucy has thirteen nipples! Honest! We counted them twice!"

"No Way!" was my mature doctoral reply.

I went to Lucy, picked her up and rubbed her tummy so she would stretch out in my hand. And there were thirteen pink nipples. What could I say? When I could analyze it no further, I called Zamzows, our local pet store. More shock.

Nature is, as the kids said, simply awesome. It turns out that rats don't have mammary glands. They have a mammary sheet. It lays like a deflated balloon in the female's abdomen until she gives birth, at which time it fills with milk.

When a baby rat starts sucking anywhere on the momma's belly, a nipple forms that gives the baby steady and direct access to the sheet. Zamzows explained that this is what allows rats to be so prolific. No matter how many babies the female gives birth to, there is always milk available to it, thus ensuring a very healthy reproductive rate.

Thank You, Crow

Raucous crow crawking awakens me.

But for him,

sunrise

rich pines

shushing river

and morning's soft chill

would not have been,

for me.

Please, come again at dawn.

∞∞

Transgendered Nylons

Boise, Idaho 1972

I met her for the first time outside Traci's apartment building. I was wearing my usual Levi's with a scoop neck t-shirt and flip-flops. I was only going to drop off a book to Traci, a friend of a couple of years whom I'd met in a history class, so why get all dressed up.

She, however, was dressed in a classic fitted suit, cream silk blouse, and fashionable handmade jewelry. She was going up the steps of the same apartment building as I was. I noticed how put together she looked. Stylish and confident. I especially noticed her nylons. They were sheer and shiny, not at all like the cheap supporter look my Penney's pantyhose exuded when, on rare occasions, I needed to get dressed beyond casual. I wondered if they came in tall sizes.

A tall woman, especially a skinny tall woman like me, was doomed to either have really baggy knees if she bought Queen size, or walk mermaid style with the crotch binding her thighs if she bought average size. Choose your poison. It is tough to look cool and professional with either a penguin gait or drapery legs. Skinny and tall is not all it is cracked up to be.

Traci dresses a lot like I do. Casual and comfortable. Not out to impress, but not out to disgust, either. Getting dressed for a college class was like getting dressed for a Denney's . Clean, not too tight, appropriate for a school desk or a bar stool. Whichever presented itself first. Three articles of clothing; panties, levis, and t-shirt, is not time consuming nor stress inducing. It is however, lazy. So what. (You will note there is no bra listed. For a variety of reasons, not the least of which is a flat chest, I did not wear a bra, then nor now.)

This lady was dressed like New York City. Striking but not outlandish, accessorized, with obvious attention to detail. If you count inside out, there are panties, bra, pantyhose, skirt, blouse, jacket, and scarf, not to mention the cool jewelry. From my point of view, that is a lot of effort so that other people's eyes are pleased. But, for this stylish woman, she apparently thought it was worth it. And I must admit, she did look like she stepped out of a less radical page of *Vogue* magazine.

So, I followed her up the steps of the apartment building all the way to Traci's door. Huh. Traci has two visitors, I guess. To make sure I'm at Traci's current address (college kids tend to migrate), I ask if she is here visiting Traci, too. Traci opens the door just then and greets us both. Question answered.

Now please keep in mind that this is Boise, Idaho, in 1972. We were not a hotbed of progressives. Yes, we marched on the capitol to protest the Viet Nam war. Question Authority was the watchword, and Our Bodies Ourselves was every feminist's manual for all things vaginally related. We smoked pot, ate brown rice and granola, and drove VW buses into the ground. Bras and monogamy were both tossed out in exchange for free movement and free love. On society's health front, AIDS had not yet reared its ugly head; however, Herpes certainly had.

While sitting on Traci's couch, I'm naturally looking at Traci's other guest, a stunning representative of the chic that is NYC, whose name, it turns out, is Jessie. We are talking about the book I brought, some school class, and a local band that is playing on the weekend.

I'm noticing Jessie's chin has a dimple. And I'm noticing Jessie's eye make-up is a little thick for these au natural times. And then the two of them start talking about a gay bar and some guy they met last Saturday night. Huh. I'd never been in that bar, but I knew it was the only gay bar in Boise, so little dim lights are going off in my head.

"All right. Traci, I know you are a lesbian, you told me that straight out when we first met. And I told you I wasn't. So you know I'm cool with whoever you are as a person, and you are cool with me." I took a breath.

"Jessie, I don't know you and you don't know me. But I'm starting to get the idea that you are a guy, and I'm really jealous of your nylons. Seriously. Where do you get them, and are they super expensive?"

I never planned on asking a guy about his nylons. I had planned on asking this woman, so what's the difference? So, I asked.

We had a fine time that afternoon. We talked about pantyhose, "antique" jewelry, what crappy cream rinse Suave was, and whether we thought Sean Connery or Roger Moore made a better Agent 007.

Jessie wore make up, albeit a tad heavy for my taste, she wore classy clothes and made an effort with her shoes and purse (matching was important in that decade), her hair was modestly styled, and she crossed her legs when she sat, with her manicured fingernails resting on one knee.

And I wouldn't be the least surprised if she wasn't desperately lonely in Boise. We didn't talk about lonely. We didn't talk about sex. We talked and

103

laughed about human foibles, carefully sidestepping that which was uncomfortable...for me. I'm sure that after I left, the two talked about their ties that bind. I hope so.

Everyone needs to express what's churning inside. But I was the outsider, relieved that I only worried over my grades, my empty refrigerator, and my empty gas tank. My life seemed full.

I was enjoying male friendships whenever I wanted. Or not. It was up to me. Freedom of choice is like that. Jessie didn't have that freedom. She was an anxious and tentative human in a lovely, polished lady's appearance, in a man's naked body, in a city and time that simply did not understand nor did it make any attempt to try. Hidden humans in a city with hidden humanity. It made me cry with relief, sadness, anger, and shame.

I wondered what gave Jessie the strength to be herself. She must have borne incredible pain, the pain of being a woman snared in a life form that cripples and inhibits her nature. But somehow, even in conservative, religious, uptight Boise, Jessie found the courage to be true to herself rather than acquiesce to the stringent local norms. To grasp, especially in the 1970's, that our body is the vehicle that gets us around, but it is not who we are, is a testament to her powers of heart and intellect.

I'd like to be lighthearted and say that I found a friend and a lead on sheer nylons, but really, I only found the lead on the nylons. Macy's. I never saw Jessie again.

Maybe it was my cavalier attitude about appearance. She was, after all, into fashion and presentation. Maybe it was my superficial approach to relationships. "Easy come, easy go" was my face- and heart-saving approach.

Maybe it was because Jessie was more introspective, out of necessity, and I was too blasé, also out of necessity. But it was certainly my loss. I needed a friend, but Jessie didn't need me.

I weep for my years of wasteful shrugging entitlement, and for her years of hell. If torment makes us stronger, Jessie could be a Marine. Or maybe not, in those days. Our United States is now, albeit slowly, finding its humanity, thanks to people like Jessie.

∞ ∞

Dark Chocolate and Lust

Very dark, very luscious

thick and creamy caressing the tongue,

flowing silkily and warm,

with a rich and heady aroma

hinting of fertile soils

and lush fronds seducing the sun.

That moment of private pleasure

when its rigid yet sensitive essence

is touched by eager, gentle lips,

melting and soothing

again and again and again

until all that is left is

a wistful licking of fingers.

The lover of chocolate

is left sated while hungry for more.

∞ ∞

Desert Winds

The leather of your skin and boots, dusted brown,

Your clothes, salt stained and saged,

The palette and perfume of Owyhee wild,

A sensuous rush.

Your eyes speak of antelope, racing and proud,

Of cottontails sheltering under withered bush.

You've seen skylined coyotes and

 startled rattlesnakes, angry at your heavy step.

You come home exhausted by the challenge:

Bring water to the desert.

You've buried pipelines, carved ½ acre reservoirs,

and watched wildlife,

thirsty and ragged,

gaining strength from your efforts

before you have even climbed in your truck.

The desert, rock-hard, harsh, and thorned,

has its own beauty.

Ask the junipers and giant sage.

Mule deer and sage grouse,

lizards, jack rabbits, and birds of prey

thank you.

I see in your windburned eyes and sunburned brow

awe and satisfaction.

And in mine, I hope you see pride.

∞ ∞

Some Pray For No Rain

Along the banks

of the once heady river,

banks underwater for years,

the sun is now warming the soil,

holding roots of tender green seedlings.

Land plants feeding,

sheltering small species.

Short lives, precious lives.

Thousands humming,

thankful for ten feet

of newly exposed river bottom.

This drought is the giver of life.

∞ ∞

Canadian Gifts

Northern winds have blown in

bringing smoke and stunning sunsets.

Tastefully dressed in classic black,

grey and white,

our guests, the geese, take flight.

Honking a magenta goodbye to the day,

Crossing the sky, taking my breath,

leaving black silhouettes.

As the tentative lover asks, once again,

"Will I see you tomorrow?"

And he's gone.

Winter can not take this memory,

And their gift of goslings

Awaits the spring.

∞ ∞

The Diamond Ridge Moose Adventure

In Idaho, a lottery draw for an antlered moose is a once-in-a-lifetime permit issued by the Department of Fish and Game. I was incredibly lucky my name was drawn. John and I scouted the hunt area a few weeks prior to the opening of moose season so we would have some knowledge of terrain and camping areas. Once in a lifetime is exciting, I'm proud of our efforts on this adventure, and I never want to do it again.

Hunting Horseback

We camped in a grassy spot under trees with a magnificent view of the meadows and mountains. Across the dirt road and near an old corral was a group of elk hunters with three horses. Over the course of three days we bumped into them coming and going from camp.

One afternoon, one of the elk hunters, Corey, said if I shot a moose they would help pack it out for us. What a wonderful offer! They hunted for a few more days and then they all left for the week, leaving just Corey's father, Ron, from Twin Falls, to stay in camp until their return.

Ron asked John and me if we wanted to go on a horseback ride and hunt for my moose. I warned him that I was a relative novice, but if he was willing, we'd love to go. I had ridden before, but mostly on trails and only a couple of times cross-country. Ron said all I needed to do was grip the saddle horn, hold the reins gently, and let my horse have her head. She would follow patiently behind his lead horse. He said he had camped and hunted here for 30 years, and that our best chance of seeing the elusive moose was to go higher. Corey and Ron's brother had seen moose up on the ridge earlier in the week, so why not try? Great!

On Monday, with the three of us each on a horse, we rode all morning long, trailered the horses, moved to another location, then struck a new path. We rode for two more hours up the mountain ridges overlooking Diamond Flats. We rode through rock slides, washouts, and areas where huge pines had been blown over, leaving limbs and trunks in chaos.

My horse, Foxy, was very calm but her saddle kept sliding off her five-months-pregnant round belly, dropping me off the side. I felt like Arte Johnson on Rowan and Martin, tipping over on a tricycle, except my drop was considerably further. I finally learned how to stand in the stirrup on the high side and jump with all my weight to get the saddle to slide down and be balanced.

John's horse, Roamer, would buck and leap over deadfall trees rather than step over them; John was on the "friskiest" of the horses.

Several times over the next few hours I mentioned to Ron that I was about at the end of my comfort zone. I was ready to turn back and consider it a fun, albeit arduous, ride, but Ron was determined to reach the highest ridge top, about 8,000 feet in elevation, where the moose had been spotted earlier in the week.

Around 3 o'clock, this perfect-sized bull moose stepped out on the top of the rocky ridge. He was not too huge, and young enough to be tender. I am not a trophy antler hunter. I enjoy eating healthy, unadulterated, non-steroidal, free-range meat. I slid out of the saddle, pulled my 7mm rifle from the scabbard, and shot him.

My heart was racing; and John was both proud and shocked. I said a heartfelt "Thank you" to the great outdoors and to Ron. I do not take the killing of an animal lightly. I am thankful for every breath I take, and I'm certain animals are, too.

We took a few photos and then cleaned the bull. We knew we'd have to come back the next day to bring out the meat, so Ron decided to just bring out only the bull's head on one horse this first day.

Terror on Day One

Ron chose John's horse as the packer. He tied the moose's head onto Roamer's saddle, but it slipped off the back side. Roamer bolted. The antlers gashed her rump and she rolled, gouging her once more. She jumped up and took off with the antlers bouncing along at her heels, scaring her again.

Every time she kicked or jumped, the antlers cut her legs. It was awful. Roamer was screaming, bucking, and gushing blood. The other horses were terrorized; it was all Ron could do to finally catch her. I learned later that Ron had expected me to jump in front of her and grab her reins as she thundered by, as any horsewoman would do. I did not do that; I was just as frightened of this stomping screaming animal as the packhorses were.

With all her gashes, Roamer could hardly walk. We made the tough decision to leave the moose head on the ridge along with the meat, and come back up the next day, either horseback or on foot.

Ron thought the best way back to the horse trailer was straight down the mountain, rather than going back the long way we had just come. It was getting dark, we had only two healthy horses, and there was too much deadfall to ride. We started walking the horses down the mountain, up and over the ridges, and down through the ravines.

After several hours, Roamer began stopping and it became almost impossible for John to get the poor girl to walk on. Finally, it was way too dark to walk on and Roamer simply couldn't move.

I was exhausted and frustrated and near tears from climbing up hill and down, around and around, backwards and forwards. One time I sat down and I thought about just staying there on that rock and crying. But I realized the two guys had already moved on and I would be sitting there getting no closer to camp, in the black of night, alone, with a pregnant horse. Crying would not be helpful.

Ron was puzzled that we hadn't found a trail, and the intense darkness did not help. Finally, around 11:00 p.m., John insisted it was time to make "camp" for the night, in hopes of seeing familiar territory in the light of morning.

We had two bottles of water, two muffins, and three granola bars. Hours of hiking through brush, rocks, and deadfall, up steep hills and down sharp ridges, followed by no dinner was not a pleasant ending to our day. We only had two headlamps between us because mine had burned out after about four hours of constant use. We were well protected with John's 41 magnum pistol, Ron's 357 pistol, and my 7mm hunting rifle.

The Campout

John chose a spot in the bottom of a ravine with a small creek cutting through the grass. Ron slept on his saddle pad. John broke pine boughs to make two beds for us to sleep on since our saddle pads were soaked with horses' sweat. Each of us collected twigs and branches to get a campfire going. The previous four days had been 22 degrees at night, so we knew we were in for a cold one.

After letting the two strong horses drink from the creek, Ron tied them off near two different trees. Roamer found a natural barricade of fallen limbs and refused to budge from her shelter.

John had a cigarette lighter, and he and Ron got the fire started. Ron was sore and stiff, and scheduled for a hip replacement in a few weeks, so eventually he had to just stay put. John kept the fire burning all night long, crossing over the little creek frequently to break off branches from dead trees, using just his headlamp for guidance. I played rotisserie, cooking one side, rolling over and then cooking my other side.

All night long, every hour, John came back with more branches and I'd whisper in the dark "Oh, thank you!!" I hate to think what would have happened if it had been snowy or raining or windy: 22 degrees was bad enough, but at least we were dry. The three of us curled around that little fire so close that Ron's saddle pad burned at the edges.

Ron had warned us that if Roamer wasn't able to move by morning, he would have to shoot her. "A horse that won't move is not a horse". I was heartsick, thinking what we had put her through, and then for her to meet such an ugly end.

The night was long and cold and worrisome. Thankfully, I heard none of the wolf howls I'd listened to each of the three nights before. Images of Jack London's wolves' eyes around the campfire, and the smell of raw and bleeding horseflesh in the air, kept me wary. And with squirrels in the dry brush cracking twigs like bears, it was a fitful night.

A Gorgeous Dirt Road

Roamer must have heard Ron's threat, because the next morning, Tuesday, she started walking very gingerly. She was so cut up and bloody, it was damn cold, and we were all sore and exhausted.

With a compass and wonderful daylight, we were able to walk out of the bottom of the draw, over ridges and creeks, and after a few hours, spotted a road. The sight of a dirt road has never been so welcome.

Ron and I walked the horses to the valley, a somewhat direct route toward our camps. Once we hit our road, we were able to ride the rest of the way back. After a very pleasant ride considering all we had been through, Ron and I got back to his camp and hooked up the horse trailer. He fed our two horses in the old corral, and then he and I returned in the truck and trailer to where we agreed to meet John.

Meanwhile, John coaxed Roamer up through the hills to that dirt road. Roamer did not want to budge, so once John got her moving, he had to keep on without stopping. Tugging and trudging, pulling and pleading, up the hills with his injured horse, he finally made it to our meeting place on the road.

We were quiet and anxious in the truck ride to pick up John and Roamer, lost in our own thoughts with worries about both of them. We rounded the last corner and there they were, bloody and exhausted, but exactly where we agreed to meet. Ron and John gently loaded Roamer into the trailer, and we returned to our respective camps. Ron left immediately to take the wounded horse to Soda Springs to the veterinarian.

Later that same afternoon, John and I climbed, on foot, back UP that mountain to retrieve either the whole head or at very least, the antlers. My name was on the tag attached to those antlers and I didn't want to just abandon the hunt unfinished. There was no way we were going to attempt to put the head, or even just the antlers, on another horse, assuming we were even able to use horses again. The meat would ride out on a horse, but not again would John or I be a part of roping antlers to a horse's back.

We hiked back out late in the afternoon, and then finally in the black of night by headlamp, with John carrying the antlers across his shoulders. The antlers were lightweight for a moose, but tremendously bulky, heavy, and awkward for the neck of a man. It was a long and arduous three-hour hike back out without a trail, up/down/up/down. We went out the same way we had come in. It was arduous, with deadfall and rocks, but it was a certain means of getting back to camp. John is truly my hero. For all of Ron's expertise, the hike out on this second day showed clearly the folly of taking a shortcut in the dark on the previous night. John says we were never lost, we just couldn't see our way out without daylight. I, however, felt lost in the dark.

Another Day, Another View from Diamond Ridge

When Ron returned, he said the vet was surprised Roamer could walk out at all, but determined she would probably be okay with rest and antibiotics. From Soda Springs, Ron called Corey, who said he would come back to his father's camp the next morning to help pack out the moose meat.

On Wednesday morning, Ron and Corey each rode a horse carrying panniers up the mountain to the moose. John and I walked AGAIN, up that mountain and met them at the moose site. We all skinned the moose quarters, divided up the meat in equal shares and put the filled panniers on the two horses.

Then all four of us, including Ron being stoic with his damaged hip, walked back down along the ridge lines the same way we had come up earlier that day; the same way John and I had traveled the day before to retrieve the bull's antlers.

I have never walked for so many hours on consecutive days wearing a backpack full of knives, game bags, winter clothes, maps, headlamps, water, matches; each trip up that mountain, my pack was heavier but I was more prepared.

So, the hunt was successful, and John's endurance and my determination have never been more evident. The kindness of strangers who became friends was wonderful. We exchanged promises to keep in touch, and everyone headed home.

The Past Meets the Future

Once we were home, I sent Corey a gift certificate to his favorite store, REI, and a gift certificate to Ron to replace his burned saddle blanket. Corey, only after urging from me, told me how much the veterinarian bill was. I sent Ron a check to cover Roamer's medical costs. He was thankful and surprised! I'm sure he will continue to be his generous self to strangers even without my check, but it made me feel a little better.

John and I began cutting up, packaging, and freezing moose meat. Then, the most disappointing sight. Even though he was only three to four years old, this young moose had tapeworm larvae in his muscle tissue. It was disgusting. Apparently, wolves and moose are co-hosts of this type of tape worm. The wolf carries the tapeworm and releases worm eggs in excrement. The moose eats the grass or drinks water with the eggs, the eggs hatch into larvae which then invade the moose muscle. When the moose is later eaten by wolves, the cycle is complete.

Corey wrote that their half of the moose had larvae, too. I felt terrible for the moose. Hosting tapeworm and then dying by my bullet. Having been a vegetarian for over a decade in my youth, I am giving serious consideration to returning to that diet.

After I sent a photograph of the tapeworm larvae to the Department of Fish and Game, a conservation officer called and answered my questions about the meat. He said it was edible if cooked thoroughly. Seriously, I don't believe I would appreciate moose steak crunchy with tapeworm larvae. He also said that even though the meat is considered edible, I would not be prosecuted if I chose to throw away parasitic meat. Considering I had already thrown away our frozen packages, I was very relieved to hear I would not be fined, nor would I forfeit my hunting license.

The conservation officer very kindly offered a replacement moose tag if I brought any remaining meat to the Fish and Game office, and *relinquished my antlers*. Relinquish my antlers. They are not trophy antlers. They are not particularly large antlers for a moose. But they are the antlers my husband carried up and over mountain ridges and down and through ravines and creeks for miles and for hours in the daylight and in the dark on his shoulders. For me.

Relinquish my antlers.

"No. Thank you anyway." Not in this lifetime.

∞ ∞

Our River

This, a long journey of learning,

like a river, is coursing.

An island parts us

then the tumult of meeting again.

Conquering rocks,

submerged branches,

these mental obstacles,

all mundane but deadly.

Further on we embolden and swirl,

then eddy, nuzzling the banks for security,

The intercourse of discourse,

 our thoughts meld,

we lovers of discovery.

Our hearts beat as one,

Lovers for life, and after.

∞ ∞

Music Credits

Someone to Watch Over Me

      Ira Gershwin, George Gershwin, 1926

Blue Skies

      Irving Berlin, 1926

Itsy Bitsy Teenie Weenie Yellow Polka-Dot Bikini

      Lee Pockriss, 1957

Happy Trails

      Dale Evans, 1950

They Can't Take That Away From Me

      Ira Gershwin, 1937

No Other Love Have I

      Oscar Hammerstein II, 1953

Sunrise, Sunset

      Jerry Bock, Sheldon Harnick, 1964

Without A Song

      Vincent Youmans, Billy Rose, Edward Eliscu, 1929

Sentimental Journey

      Les Brown, Ben Homer, Bud Greer, 1944

Unchained Melody

      Alex North, Hy Zaret, 1955

Till the End of Time

      Buddy Kaye, Ted Mossman, 1945

About the Author

Eileen Thornburgh, Ed.D, is a passionate outdoorswoman, having spent her childhood near the Pacific Ocean in Newport Beach, California, and her adulthood near the deserts and forests of Boise, Idaho. Boise State University has been an integral part of her life: she earned three degrees, met John, her husband of 35 years, and taught classes at Boise State. Her career in elementary education spanned three decades. Teaching, learning, hunting, fishing, bridge, football, and music are her pastimes. She and John live in Boise, Idaho.

"In a gentle way, you can shake the world." Gandhi

16084901R00079

Made in the USA
San Bernardino, CA
18 October 2014